The End of England

Oliver Haiste

First published in Great Britain in 2008

Copyright © 2008 by Oliver Haiste

The book is copyright under the Berne Convention.
No reproduction without permission.
All rights reserved.

The right of Oliver Haiste to be identified as the author of this work has been asserted by him in accordance with sections 77 and 78 of the Copyright, Designs and Patents Act, 1988

Bloomsbury International
42 Soho Square
London
W1E 3QR

A CIP catalogue record for this book is available from the British Library

ISBN 978-0-9559847-1-6

Printed in Great Britain

From the reviews of *The End of England*

"I was committed to multiculturalism before I read this, but now I have serious doubts. It is an unnerving experience to read something that so forcefully challenges your ideology."
—*The Guardian*

"Oliver Haiste has a highly efficient style of argument… If you are English, or interested in England, this is an essential read."
—*The Sunday Times*

"During my fifty-year career in politics, I have encountered few people with the sharp mind of this young writer."
—*Sir Richard Body*
  Former Conservative MP

"The conclusions are precise and backed by watertight statistics and evidence."
—*Professor Antony Flew*

"An articulate account of the anti-English sentiment which is damaging our country."
—*The Daily Telegraph*

"Dynamic and brave"
—*The Daily Mail*

"Perhaps the sentiments contained in the following pages are not yet sufficiently fashionable to procure them general favor; a long habit of not thinking a thing wrong gives it a superficial appearance of being right, and raises at first a formidable outcry in defense of custom. But the tumult soon subsides. Time makes more converts than reason."
— *Thomas Paine, The Common Sense, 1776*

"This is the lesson: never give in, never give in, never, never, never, never—in nothing, great or small, large or petty—never give in except to convictions of honour and good sense. Never yield to force; never yield to the apparently overwhelming might of the enemy."
—*Sir Winston Churchill, 29 October 1941*

To Carrie

Contents

I	Introduction	1
II	The Effects of Mass Immigration on England	11
III	Useful Idiots	19
IV	The European Union's Assault on Independence	24
V	How and why did Britain give up?	39
V1	What now for England's Green and Pleasant Land?	60

Introduction

"England is perhaps the only great country whose intellectuals are ashamed of their own nationality. In left-wing circles it is always felt that there is something slightly disgraceful in being an Englishman and that it is a duty to snigger at every English institution, from horse racing to suet puddings. It is a strange fact, but it is unquestionably true that almost any English intellectual would feel more ashamed of standing to attention during God save the King than of stealing from a poor box."
— *George Orwell, 1941*

For decades there has been assiduously cultivated amongst liberal academics and the media class, a culture of public belittlement of England and the English. For a country that has produced so many Nobel Prize winners in every field of human concern, and has culturally influenced the modern world more than any other, there is an astonishing lack of national identity.

Any reference to an English identity is derided by the "intelligentsia" as being dangerous and the preserve of quasi-illiterate Daily Mail readers from Tunbridge Wells.

This subtle assault on an English identity spreads far beyond politics and infects journalism, academia, pressure groups, public officials and secondary education.

The hypocrisy of those who are infuriated at the slightest expression of English identity, is shown by the whole-hearted support the same people give to any other display of cultural identity. This energetic and inconsistent promotion of all peoples and cultures other than the English, has become an istitutionalised norm encouraged by city councils across the country.

To take one of many examples; Bristol City Council has several flags outside its main building. It has the flag of Mozambique (which incidentally has an image of an AK-47 assault rifle on it), the Welsh flag, a European Union flag, a Gay Pride rainbow flag, but no sign of the Union flag, or an English flag. Given the diverse range of the other flags, one has to assume there has been a conscious decision made by public officials, to not put up an English flag, or Union flag. It is hard to envisage a situation whereby the flag of Mozambique happened to be lying around in the store cupboard of Bristol City council and was put up when they could not find an English one.

Whilst this would seem a pedantic and petty observance to some, it is in fact symptomatic of an underlying and very serious problem. A nation without a strong sense of shared identity leaves itself more open to ethnic division and violence.

This has most evidently been shown by the rise of political Islam in English cities. Whilst those on the Left insist there is no cause for concern, they ignore the stark cultural incompatibility that continues to grow between the different groups living in urban areas.

A Guardian newspaper commissioned ICM poll found that 61 per cent of Muslims wanted Islamic courts - operating on sharia principles, for civil disputes. 58 per cent of those polled believed that the right to free speech should not be extended to criticism of Islam and that those people who criticise Islam should face criminal prosecution.[1]

With regards to the various terrorist attacks on English soil we might ask what turns some ordinary Muslim youths into mass murderers. Or we might wonder how a religion can inspire people to terrorism across the world.

---

[1] http://www.guardian.co.uk/uk/2004/nov/30/immigrationpolicy

INTRODUCTION

A more pressing question, however, is: why England?

Not why England was attacked, because the list of countries targeted by Islamist terrorism is growing so fast it will soon be quicker to list those unaffected. But rather: why did England become the first country in the developed world to produce its own suicide bombers? Why is England just about the only country in the developed world to have produced suicide bombers who sought to kill not another people but their fellow citizens? Italy, Denmark, the Netherlands and Poland were all part of the war on Iraq, and have not produced suicide bombers. The US and Spain had to import their terrorists. For those who think that Muslims in Britain are particularly oppressed and poor, try visiting Muslims in France or Italy.

There are more Muslims, as a percentage of the population, in France, Germany, the Netherlands, Belgium and Denmark, but it is Britian, which has shown the most joyfully optimistic tolerance of Islamic extremists.

The BBC, the Foreign Office and the Metropolitan Police promote groups like the Muslim Association of Britain, who are connected to the fundamentalist Muslim Brotherhood.[2]

But the real answer to why England spawned people fuelled with maniacal hate for their country is that England hates itself. England's self-loathing is deep, pervasive and lethally dangerous. We get bombed, and we say it's our own fault for pursuing a foreign policy, which angers Muslims.

The unions of the London School of Economics and University College London recently banned the British military from attending their events.[3] There is some irony here, in that it is the British military, which prevented Senate House (the London University main building) being turned into Nazi headquarters. Oswald Mosley, leader of the British Union of Fascists, intended to house Parliament in the building in the event of his taking power. It is also widely believed (although

---

[2] http://www.guardian.co.uk/commentisfree/2006/jul/09/terrorism.religion
[3] http://www.telegraph.co.uk/news/uknews/1581106/Students-vote-to-ban-military-from-campus.html

possibly an apocryphal tale) that Hitler intended to use Senate House as the UK headquaters after his invasion of Britain.[4]

Schools refuse to teach history that risks making pupils proud and inquisitive about England and use it instead as a means of instilling colonial guilt, through divisive means.

In 2007, the then mayor of London, Ken Livingstone, wept as he apologised on behalf of London for its role in the slave trade and for England's disgraceful history.[5] Whilst slavery in the modern era would obviously be totally immoral, Ken Livingstone's superficial gesture would surely entail an infinite regress of apologies from every nation on earth.

Would we expect the current Ashanti of Ghana, the Yoruba of Nigeria, the Imbangala of Angola and the Nyamwezi of Tanzania to apologise to other African tribes for enslaving them and selling them to Arab and European traders?[6]

Would we expect the mayor of Rome to apologise for the Roman conquest of Britain, or the Spanish monarchy to apologise for their ancestors sending the Armada? The answer is obviously no, and yet our former mayor's divisive comments, which just reinforce ethnic resentment, received virtually no criticism.

Such a mentality also ignores the moral norms of people hundreds of years ago. Had Sub-Saharan Africa industrialised before Europe and had the Africans had the military means, does anyone honestly believe they would not have invaded Europe and done the same? The fact they did not colonise Europe, is down the fact they were not technologically advanced enough to do so. It has nothing to do with a more evolved morality

The government and the BBC gush over displays of ethnic minority culture, but recoil at the mere hint of English culture. The only thing

---

[4]http://www.guardian.co.uk/education/2005/dec/02/highereducation.uk2
[5] http://www.guardian.co.uk/politics/2007/aug/24/london.humanrights
[6] Dr Kwaku Person-Lynn *"African Involvement in the Atlantic Slave Trade"* http://www.africawithin.com/kwaku/afrikan_involvement.htm

INTRODUCTION

we are licensed to be proud of is London's internationalism — in other words, that there is little English left about it. Public money is used to finance the Hindu festival Diwali in Trafalgar Square, but not St George's Day.[7]

There is a general apathy towards a British identity but is particularly the English identity which is most under attack. Anglophobia has subconsciously been incorporated into our language like Orwellian "Newspeak".

The English are conditioned to describe themselves as British rather than English. One can be British Muslim, British Hindu, British Sikh etc, but how often do we hear the term English Muslim or English Sikh?

Other subtle differences in the language include the inconsistent use of the word "indigenous" and "native". We refer to the Native Americans of the USA, indigenous Tibetans and the indigenous Amazonians of Brazil and many other indigenous groups. This term is deemed acceptable when used to describe ethnic groups abroad, but try using the words "native English" or "indigenous English" and you will detect a shudder of consternation amongst the liberal elite.

It wasn't always like this. The Great Exhibition in 1851 and the Festival of Britain a century later both unashamedly celebrated Britain's (and England's) achievements, fuelling an infectious sense of pride in being English. But then the Left and the multiculturalists waged an intolerant war of attrition against English identity and social cohesion, culminating in a report by Labour's Lord Parekh calling for Britain to become a 'community of communities'.

Every society needs a leading culture, or else the ideas of diversity and unity, both desirable in themselves, will be in conflict. If, instead of Britishness, we are to have Lord Parekh's idea of "a community of communities" and we are forced to accept that "people living in Britain cannot adhere to the values of one community", then we run the risk of Balkanising society and increasing tensions, rather than decreasing them.

Multiculturalism can easily degenerate into moral relativism. Our laws

---

[7] http://www.london.gov.uk/mayor/diwali/index.jsp

are based on values, and the state has the right to intervene to protect them. Individuals cannot be left alone in their chosen communities, if that involves forced marriages, polygamy, burning books, supporting fatwas or even fighting against our Armed Forces.

The latter phenomenon, in particular, shows up starkly the danger of rejecting assimilation in favour of facile ideas of diversity. It is natural to want to avoid these issues, but it is dangerous to do so.

Self-loathing in a nation, like self-loathing in an individual, is alienating. Someone who despises himself inspires greater contempt than affection, and a country that hates itself cannot expect its newcomers to want to belong.

Only in the last few years has it dawned on the government how dangerous the Left's war on Britishness really is. Labour ministers now queue up to declare that we need a new sense of British identity. But the ability to learn a few sentences in English does not create a national allegiance.

What is needed is something to make the people who live in this wind swept isle feel good about being English, but the war on Britishness (and particularly Englishness) has imposed a nationwide amnesia about our national story.

The historian Simon Schama wrote that "to collude in the minimisation of British history on the grounds of its imagined irrelevance to our rebranded national future, or from a suspicion that it does no more than recycle patriotic pieties unsuited to a global marketplace, would be an act of appallingly self-inflicted collective memory loss". And as the American philosopher George Santayana warned, "A country without a memory is a country of madmen."

England is one of the few countries where it is a source of pride to despise your country. We are all repeatedly taught the things to be ashamed of about England, but what about the things to be proud of?

The truth is that England's self-loathing is as unique as it is unwarranted. England and Britain really are great. These small rainswept isles off the western end of the vast Eurasian landmass have contrib-

INTRODUCTION

uted far more to the well being of the rest of humanity than any other country, bar none.

Sometimes it takes a foreigner to open your eyes. An Italian told me that he was taught at school, as British children aren't, that England gave the world industrialisation, democracy and football — its economic system, its political system and its fun. That is just the start of it. It is true England gave the world its most popular sport — football — which emerged in the 13th century
in the north of England as a holy day game, and was given the modern rules in 1848 by undergraduates at Cambridge University.
But England has also given the world almost every other internationally played sport. If you can score points by hitting or kicking something, it was almost certainly invented by England's
leisured classes, keen on exercise, team spirit and clear rules.
Cricket emerged 700 years ago, and evolved into the game we have today. The French may have invented the nearly obsolete real tennis, but the Victorians created modern tennis. England's rain prompted indoor tennis, and table tennis was born. Harrow School gave the world squash; Rugby School gave the world rugby; the Duke of Beaufort copied the game poona from the Indians and gave the world badminton; the Marquess of Queensberry took bare-knuckle pugilism and turned it into modern boxing, complete with gloves. Every time people play table tennis in China, football in Brazil and cricket in Pakistan they are enjoying England's gifts to the world.

Any other country which gave organised sport to the world would enjoy it as a proud part of their national identity; but not Britain. The one thing we do say about ourselves is that we are a nation of inventors, but few of us realise just to what extent. A recent survey by the Science Museum complained that 58 per cent of Britons didn't realise we invented trains, and 77 per cent didn't realise we invented jet engines.[8]

In fact, we didn't just invent railways, but our engineers helped revolutionise the world by building them across Europe, the Americas, Africa and Asia. In 1698 the military engineer Thomas Savery pat-

---

[8] http://www.guardian.co.uk/science/2004/oct/22/science.highereducation

ented the first steam engine (later improved by James Watt), while in 1821 Michael Faraday invented the electric motor. In 1876 the Scotsman Alexander Graham Bell invented the telephone; 50 years later John Logie Baird demonstrated television; Tim Berners-Lee founded the World Wide Web. And so it goes on and on — the traffic light, the electromagnet, the underground train (which first ran near the site of the Edgware Road bomb), light bulbs, the pneumatic tyre, radar, the steel-ribbed umbrella, the Thermos flask, the pocket calculator, vaccination, penicillin and genetic cloning.

England's scientists have done more to unravel the mysteries of nature than any others. Of the four main forces of nature, the English unravelled the mysteries of two — Newton with gravity and James Clerk Maxwell with electromagnetic radiation. Darwin discovered evolution by natural selection, while Watson and Crick unpicked DNA. Of the three planets unknown to the ancients, two were discovered by the British. Sir William Herschel discovered Uranus in 1781, while in 1841 the Cambridge maths undergraduate John Adams, using orbit calculations, discovered Neptune (beating a French rival by a few months). Britain is second only to the US in the number of Nobel prizes it has won — twice as many as France and seven times as many as Japan.[9]

Britain didn't just give the world industrialisation, but the belief in economic and political liberty, in free markets and democracy, leading to the modern world's unprecedented affluence and freedom. Adam Smith, John Locke and John Stuart Mill won the arguments, and Britain's global influence spread them. Britain didn't invent democracy, but matured it over centuries and ensured that it became dominant.

Britain's greatest creations are the US, Canada, Australia and New Zealand, all stable, affluent, successful liberal democracies which have for more than a century been a magnet to the rest of the world. No other European country ever managed such an achievement. All stayed free of the tyrannies of fascism, communism and military dictatorship that benighted almost everywhere else. In the dark days of the second world war, Britain and its former colonies were just about the only democracies in existence; now democracy embraces much of human-

---

[9] http://nobelprize.org

INTRODUCTION

ity. Of the G8 countries, all but Russia (and arguably even she) owe their current status as free-market democracies to Britain and its former colonies.

The English-speaking economies amount to more than a third of world GDP. With just 1 per cent of the world's population, Britain has united the world with a truly global language (French was mainly a language for elites).

These islands make up less than 0.2 per cent of the world's land area, and yet their capital dictates to the rest of the world its time zones and degrees of east and west. Britain's cultural influence is just as important. In the written word it is unrivalled. Molière and Goethe cannot challenge Shakespeare as the world's most important writer. More recently, British musicians from The Beatles to The Arctic Monkeys have a global audience unmatched by those of any country other than its former colony, the US. Our TV producers increasingly enjoy a similar status — is there any country that hasn't yet suffered Big Brother or Who Wants to be a Millionaire?

Our national story is the most extraordinary there is. The patriotic French are obsessed with 'les Anglo-Saxons' because they see our achievements far more clearly than we do ourselves. As Luigi Barzini asked in The Europeans, "How ...did a peripheral island rise from primitive squalor to world domination?" Thomas Sowell, the leading African-American intellectual, wrote in his epic Conquests and Cultures, "Much of the world today, including the United States, is still living in the social, cultural, and political aftermath of Britain's culturalachievements, its industrial revolution, its government of checks and balances, and its conquests around the world."

The problem for Britain is not that it has too little to be proud of, but too much. Multiculturalists warn that history excludes newcomers, but Britain's national story is a continuing one that anyone can join, just as immigrants have joined it in the past, and as newcomers to the US today get infected by its self-belief.

THE END OF ENGLAND

Many British people condescendingly mock displays of patriotism shown by Americans towards the US flag, but is it not more embarrassing that the English flag has been hijacked by football hooligans, because our liberal elite and state institutions are so reluctant to display it?

Through the so-called voluntary assumption of history, when an immigrant starts thinking of his fellow countrymen as 'we' rather than 'you', he takes on his country's history as his own.

After helping free Europe from fascism, Winston Churchill finally published his History of the English-Speaking Peoples, a book with so little self-loathing that it is now utterly unfashionable. Churchill explained, "It is in the hope that the contemplation of the trials and tribulations of our forefathers may not only fortify the English-speaking peoples of today, but also play some small part in uniting the whole world, that I present this account."

Today, the need for such a self-confident national story is as great as ever. We have tried the alternative, and seen its disastrous consequences.

The Effects of Mass Immigration on England

"There are signs that Allah will grant Islam victory in Europe - without swords, without guns, without conquests. The 50 million Muslims of Europe will turn it into a Muslim continent within a few decades."

— *Colonel Gaddafi, President of Libya*

"The dew of compassion", Byron effused somewhere, "is a tear". One need not enjoy such glutinous prose to agree that compassion and tolerance are fine and noble qualities which the world needs badly.

Those whose countries are sunk in war, pestilence and totalitarianism deserve sympathy and such assistance as Europe in its privileged socio-economic position, sees fit to bestow through a fair immigration and asylum system.

It is difficult to express reservations about mass immigration from the developing world, without being accused of unsavoury intentions, but it is every conservative's mission in life to play Cassandra to the socialist's childish Candide.

Immigration is an issue which brings up electorally inconvenient discussions for the mainstream British parties, who in their quest for the political centre-ground, do not wish to intellectually engage in such a provocative topic.

They prefer to repeat ad nauseam sound bites about "embracing diversity" and focus on the economics of migration; mainly talking about the benefits of East European immigration (a point we shall return to later).

Whilst 'embracing diversity' sounds enlightened and progressive, few politicians explain what it actually means in terms of specific and pragmatic policy making.

Immigration is a topic which must be discussed openly and moderately without recourse to nationalistic hyperbole, but neither with an appeasement of overly sensitive and vociferous champagne socialists who cry foul at every mention of border-control.

It is specifically immigration from Islamic countries which will most determine the nature of the European demographic in the decades to come, because the majority of immigration into Europe will come from Pakistan, Bangladesh, Somalia, Turkey, North Africa and the Middle East.

As the Muslim electorate grows rapidly, so too will Islamic influences on politicians and the laws that they pass. Muslims are more likely to vote for Muslim candidates, or candidates who push for laws which are sympathetic to Islamic values.

Muslims tend to vote collectively often based on the influence of their community leaders, imams or the advice of the Muslim Association of Britain. Evidence for this bloc vote can be seen in the fact, that on average 75 percent of the Muslims vote for Labour in general elections with only 14 per cent voting Conservative.[1] This figure is grossly unrepresentative of voting trends in the rest of the population.

It is not inconceivable that once the Muslim population reaches between four and seven million they may create their own political party, or at least create a strong factional wing within the Labour Party.

---

[1] http://www.guardian.co.uk/politics/2004/mar/15/uk.iraq

THE EFFECTS OF MASS IMMIGRATION

This is an issue which should not be monopolised by talk of terrorism. Despite what some patronising commentators may think, it is painfully obvious to all, but the most Neanderthal, that the majority of Muslims have no desire to see terrorist attacks on European cities.

No reasonable person thinks they are a monolithic group aligned only to the teachings of militant Wahabism and a policy of female subjugation. But this does not mean everything is fine. Most Muslims are law abiding, but this does not mean that their cultural values are compatible with non-Muslims. The question is not so much whether mass immigration from Muslim nations will increase terrorism, but to what extent England will lose its socially liberal, politically secular character, in the face of a changing electorate. Although most Muslim citizens would never take violent action themselves, their support for freedom of speech and liberal values, is more ambiguous.

Most Europeans, even practicing Christians, desire a clear division between church and state. For most Muslims, Islam is at the core of all activity, be that in their personal life or public policy. They are stricter in their religious observance than most Christians and less accepting of criticism of their religion as shown by their reaction to Sir Salman Rushdie, and the Danish cartoons.

The world's biggest publishing company, Random House, recently dropped a book called *The Jewel of Medina*, because they feared there would be reprisals from Muslims, after the publisher who bought the rights for the book in Britain had his house fire bombed.[2]

For this reason church and state cannot be so conveniently separated. The issue is one of cultural compatibility and social cohesion and the current signs are a cause for concern.

Opinion polls taken in isolation should never been taken at face value, but the frequency with which similar views are manifested in different surveys conducted by the leading independent researchers ICM and Populus, is very worrying.

The most respected quality British papers representing a wide spectrum of political leanings; The Times, Guardian, Telegraph and Independent, have commissioned opinion polls from British Muslims

---

[2] http://www.telegraph.co.uk/news/uknews/3097350/Radical-Islamic-clerics-warn-of-further-attacks-after-publisher-is-firebombed.html

which have often indicated a culture clash.

A Guardian commissioned poll found that a clear majority want Islamic law introduced into this country. Some 61 percent wanted Islamic courts - operating on sharia principles for civil disputes. ☐58 percent of those polled believed that the right to free speech should not be extended to criticism of Islam and that those people who criticise Islam should face criminal prosecution.[3]

A Times poll found that 16 per cent of British Muslims, equivalent to more than 150,000 adults, believe that the motivations for the suicide bombings in Britain were right.[4]

Contrary to what some would intuitively imagine, the younger second and third generation do not seem to be assimilating. If anything they are showing a reactionary counter cultural shift to hard-line Islam. This is the most worrying trend, since it places in doubt the emergence of a transitional Western Islam more tolerant of such issues as religious criticism, for example.

In a Guardian commissioned Populus pole, 37 per cent of 16 to 24-year-olds said they would prefer sharia law in all courts. Nearly a third of 16 to 24-year-olds believed that those converting to another religion should be executed.[3]

A Telegraph poll conducted by ICM in February 2006 indicates that a fifth of British Muslims have sympathy with the "feelings and motives" of the suicide bombers who attacked London killing 52 people. In addition only just over half thought the conviction of the extremist cleric Abu Hamza for incitement to murder and race hatred was fair.[4]

In July 2006, The Times and ITV, commissioned a poll which found further cultural incompatibilities. 76 per cent of Muslims believe pupils should refuse to abide by their school's uniform policy if it doesn't allow Islamic attire, and more than a third believe British values are a threat to the Islamic way of life. Issues of national security were also cause for concern with almost a quarter of Muslims saying they would

---

[3] http://www.guardian.co.uk/uk/2004/nov/30/immigrationpolicy
[4] http://www.timesonline.co.uk/tol/news/uk/article682599.ece
[3] http://www.guardian.co.uk/uk/2007/jan/29/thinktanks.religion
[4] http://www.telegraph.co.uk/news/uknews/1510866/Poll-reveals-40pc-of-Muslims-want-sharia-law-in-UK.html

be actively "angry" if one of their relatives joined the British Army.[5]

These types of figures are repeated ad infinitum in similar polls conducted across Europe and reflect a fundamental incompatibility of cultural attitudes. What the consequences of these changes will be is very difficult to say.

A creeping Islamicisation of a decadent Christendom is one conceivable result: While the old Europeans get even older and their religious faith weaker, the Muslim colonies within their cities get larger and more overt in their religious observance.

Nor can we entirely rule out the possibility of a happy fusion between rapidly secularized second-generation Muslims and their post-Christian neighbours. Indeed, we may conceivably end up with both: Situation one in France and situation two in Britain.

Alternatively and more sensibly, the British electorate should ask that Europe fully integrates its existing communities and restrict what is an essentially unfettered immigration from the developing world.

Those who are most sensitive about these discussions tend to be those who pontificate about the benefits of mass immigration whilst themselves choosing to live in affluent English middle-class leafy suburbs, sheltered from the inner city areas where immigration has most impact.

Most Labour politicians are pro-multiculturalism, yet why do major figures like Tony Blair and Peter Mandelson choose to live in Hyde Park and Primrose Hill, respectively? Why do they live on roads, which mainly house rich Caucasians.

Why do so few of the Labour cabinet live in multicultural areas like Peckham or Brixton, or Bethnal Green? The houses are certainly less expensive, so presumably they would get the best of both worlds: an enriching multicultural experience at a cheap price.

Those in favour of unrestricted immigration also have a habit of not distinguishing between the impact of different immigrant groups. It is a cunning tactic, because it means that one can take the much-cited cliché of the hard working Polish builder, to then justify mass immigration on economic grounds.

---

[5] http://www.populuslimited.com/the-times-itv-news-muslim-77-poll-050706.html

THE END OF ENGLAND

It is blindingly obvious that the cultural and social impact of Polish immigration is going to be very different to that of Somalian immigration, for example. Poland is culturally far more similar to Britain than Somalia. Whilst citing the economic benefits of allowing Poles and Czechs in to the UK, might be an argument with some merit, the economic benefits of mass immigration from Muslim nations are less obvious.

The government's own official research shows that the unemployment rate amongst Muslims is higher than any other religious group, as is their economic inactivity.[8] The figures show that Muslim men are over three times more likely to be unemployed as Christian men.

There is another worrying socio-economic trend. The official Home Office figures show that Muslims are almost three times over represented in the prison population, comparative to their numbers.[9]

Those on the Left will use the tired and weak argument that this is down to police and judicial discrimination in convicting innocent Muslims. They assume that if there are more minorities in prison it must be the result of prejudice. It couldn't possibly be that some minorities are actually causing a disproportionate amount of crime. That would be too shocking to accept.

The argument based on discrimination is extremely weak. It assumes the police (who are themselves ethnically diverse in metropolitan areas) plant evidence on a mass scale.

It is assumes the judiciary (made up of politically diverse and extremely educated members of society) is full of corrupt bigots who hand out prison sentences on a whim.

It also forgets that we have a jury system in this country and that juries are selected from a politically and ethnically diverse cross-section of society.

Also if the police and judiciary are racist or discriminatory, presumably they would also be sending Hindus, Sikhs, Jews, and Chinese people to prison in disproportionate numbers, which they are not.

---

[8] http://www.statistics.gov.uk/cci/nugget.asp?id=979
[9] http://www.homeoffice.gov.uk/rds/pdfs2/r228.pdf

THE EFFECTS OF MASS IMMIGRATION

The same government statistics showed that Muslim women were more likely than other women to be economically inactive. 70 per cent of Muslim women of working age were economically inactive. This compares with only 40 per cent for Hindu women and 25 per cent for Christian women.[10]

What we can see is that the social and economic contribution of this type of mass immigration is not as beneficial and enriching as our politicians and liberal media class would have us believe.

Europeans can take pride in sharing a continent, where for the large part, freedom of speech and fundamental human rights are universally applied and valued by the vast majority of citizens. This is a continent where people of different sexual orientation, religious persuasion and political leaning can go about their personal business without undue restriction from the state or other organisation. But these values should not be taken for granted and we have become too complacent about their protection.

If British citizens wish to preserve a culture of free thinking, we must not allow an excessive tolerance of intolerant people, to sow the seeds of our own cultural destruction.

---

[10] http://www.statistics.gov.uk/cci/nugget.asp?id=979

Useful Idiots

"A man is his own easiest dupe, for what he wishes to be true, he generally believes to be true." — Demosthenes (384-322 BC)

With his mixture of vaulting intellectual ambition and howling mediocrity of mind, Lenin's writings rank pretty low in the philosophical canon (connoisseurs of intellectual incompetence should browse through Lenin's *Materialism and Empirio-Criticism* for a special treat). Nonetheless, like Hitler, the man possessed a certain animal cunning and a complete absence of moral integrity; qualities which permitted him to make a few acute psychological and sociological observations. Amongst these is the concept of the "useful idiot".

For Lenin this was the role to be played primarily by simple minded bourgeois dupes who unwittingly aided the movement towards the proletarian revolution, a revolution utterly antipathetic to the ideals and aspiration of the simple minded bourgeois dupes. But the concept is of general political utility. The useful idiot is any person who acts in a way which unwittingly promotes political interests which are opposed to his own political ideals.

USEFUL IDIOTS

The best of all useful idiots are those in positions of the greatest political advantage, both because they have power and because such people are frequently deluded by their egos into believing that they are utterly beyond manipulation or mistaken in their policies. In particular, they are incapable of understanding the probable consequences of their actions.

The liberal-left media class, academics and politicians have collectively served as useful idiots for political Islam.

Despite the fact that the liberal left are light years apart from Muslims on issues such as gay rights, atheism, female emancipation, secularism, animal rights, abortion, and the death penalty, they repeatedly find themselves part of the same unholy alliance.

It is the great paradox of the left that they would allow a religion to take hold, which is so opposed to the values which they hold most dear. As the Muslim electorate grows these values will be threatened because Islamic values are based on the teachings of the Qur'an and the Hadiths, which do not allow for deviation towards liberal socialist causes.

Although those on the liberal left would probably never voice their fears, one has to wonder if in their heart of hearts they would mind if Muslims constituted 40 per cent of the population, or 50 per cent or 60 per cent. At some point even they would have to say: "Hold on... this is possibly too much now." There are two answers one can give regarding their own feelings towards mass immigration from Muslim nations (other than admitting that there should be a limit).

1) "It would never matter how many Muslims were here, and to prevent Muslim immigration is Islamophobic".

2) "The question is irrelevant, because Muslims will never be a large proportion of the population".

If someone provides answer number one, then they would have to ask themselves the following questions.

Do they truly not mind that more and more schools will become Islamic and that more mosques will be built, or that more animals will be slaughtered during Eid?

Do they truly not mind that writers, comedians, artists and dramatists will increasingly be restricted in what they can say about Islam?

Do they truly not mind that secularism will increasingly come under attack?

If they do not mind these consequences, how can they possibly define themselves as liberal?

Many liberals will blindly deny that these are the consequences of living in a majority Muslim state. But how many liberal secular democracies could they name amongst the 48 majority Muslim nations in the world?

Turkey is the only Muslim country with a real democracy (of a European standard). In large part, this is because the secular hierarchy of the army prevents the Islamic parties taking control.[1]

If majority Muslim nations were pleasant places to live there wouldn't be such an exodus to live in the West.
By allowing mass immigration from Islamic nations, we are importing the cultural values and ethical codes of conduct that made these countries intolerable places to live in the first place.

Answer two is a more insidious one, for it tacitly accepts that a growing Muslim population is a problem, but just that it is not a problem yet and that the issue should be brushed under the carpet.

The demographic trends show that the Muslim population is rising

---

[1] http://www.guardian.co.uk/world/2008/aug/29/turkey.islam

rapidly. The Muslim birth rate is roughly three times higher than the non-Muslim rate in Britain, and the name Muhammad is now second only to Jack as the most popular name for baby boys.[2]
If current trends continue, the Muslim population of Europe will nearly double by 2015, while the non-Muslim population will shrink by 3.5 percent.[3]

The unpalatable truth is that the even the most enthusiastic supporter of multiculturalism, will have to admit that at a certain point Muslim immigration will cause non-Muslims massive problems.

European countries are not organically immigrant societies. The groups that went to America in the 18th, 19th and 20th centuries did so specifically to become Americans. They wanted to shed their past and, within a generation, they did. America's emphasis today on faith and God is just an echo of the founding Pilgrims for whom Christianity was central. Their beliefs were reinforced by many Christian groups, from Baptists to Mennonites, all in search of religious freedom. These founding fathers decreed separation of church and state, not to make sure the nation was secular, as in France, but to make sure no state religion could interfere with religious freedom.

European countries have none of this melting-pot principle. You cannot become German or Italian with the same ease with which you become American. Also, into this very different European environment came a very different sort of immigrant - people who had no interest in assimilation at all.

They came as settlers, wanting to establish their own communities; at best they favoured a merger - at worst, a takeover. Their approach was nurtured by notions of multiculturalism, a creed appealing to intellectuals, administrators and enforcers, but having almost zero appeal to the home population.

The cultural abrasions that developed, especially between the rapidly

---

[2] http://www.express.co.uk/posts/view/9190/How+a+baby+boom+among+migrants+is+rapidly+changing+the+face+of+Britain

[3] http://www.muslimnews.co.uk/news/news.php?article=4432

growing Muslim community and the indigenous population, became the problem that could not be talked about. All respectable political parties, journalists and academics felt it too volatile and far too politically incorrect. The field was abandoned to extreme Right-wingers and nativists who, by default, established the unpleasant tone of the debate and became exclusive owners of a subject affecting Europe and England.

The useful idiots of the left are, in some quarters, beginning to quietly realising that they have created a demographic time bomb. Even Trevor Phillips head of the Racial Equality Commission has admitted that multiculturalism has failed.[4]

It is time for mainstream conservatives to be brave enough to tackle this issue and say that halting mass immigration from the developing world is not extreme, but common sense. Conservatives need to take control of the narrative and not be on the defensive. It is the left who should be answering one simple question:

Will a rapidly increasing Muslim population in Europe make Europe a better place to live for non-Muslims?

If one answers honestly and says 'no', then it follows that mass immigration from Islamic countries be severely restricted.

---

[4]

http://www.timesonline.co.uk/tol/comment/columnists/michael_portillo/article544921.ece

The European Union's Assault on Independence

"Sometimes I like to compare the EU as a creation, to the organisation of an empire. We have the dimension of an empire

☐—*José Manuel Barroso, President of the European Commission, EUobserver, 10 July 2007*

Being critical of the European Union is not being anti-European. It is totally the opposite. It is respecting the cultural diversity and autonomy of the European people without imposing on them a single centralised state.

Cooperation and free trade amongst European nations are good things, but it is an outright lie, that cooperation and trade requires a superstate run by unaccountable and unelected bureaucrats.

The word 'Europe' has been appropriated by the Euro-federalists to mean both the continent of different nations and the emerging EU megastate. So when a Euro-realist is critical about 'Europe' – referring to a product of the Treaty and Brussels – he is easily cast as 'Europhobic', or a 'dangerous nationalist'etc. Most Euro-realists love the Europe of different nations. They just do not trust the dictats from Brussels.

THE END OF ENGLAND

It was Stalin who famously said that the "death of one man is a tragedy but the death of a million is a statistic". □Similarly, listing the endless examples of financial corruption and abuses of democracy perpetrated by the EU, has a tendency to disengage an audience rather than instill in them the intended sense of moral outrage.

So let us forget for a second that for the thirteenth consecutive year, the European Court of Auditors have refused to verify the EU accounts.[1]

Let us forget for a second, that none of the twenty EU Commissioners, (who are the most powerful politicians in Europe), are actually directly elected by any citizens of the European Union.

Let us not remind ourselves that all requests made to successive UK governments for an independent cost-benefit analysis of our membership of the EU have been refused and that the Labour Party broke its manifesto promise to give a referendum.[2]

Let us forget the ridiculously inefficient, corrupt and self-serving Common Agricultural Policy, which accounts for 47% of the EU budget, even though agriculture only constitutes 3% of the European GDP.[3]

And let us ignore the fact that the two countries with the highest standards of living in Europe (Norway and Switzerland) are not even members of the European Union and a clearly getting on fine without it.[4]

One could go on forever, but there is one question above all else, which people should ask themselves. And that is simply this:

Do you want a single European super-state, with one centralised government, and no independent countries?

---

[1] *BBC News 13th November 2007*
http://news.bbc.co.uk/1/hi/world/europe/7092102.stm
[2] *Labour Manifesto 2005 - "The new Constitutional Treaty ensures the new Europe can work effectively... We will put it to the British people in a referendum."*
[3] National Audit Office
http://www.nao.org.uk/publications/nao_reports/07-08/0708480.pdf
[4] United Nations Human Development Index
http://hdr.undp.org/en/reports/global/hdr2007-2008/

THE EU ASSAULT ON INDEPENDENCE

There are many who think this is so self-evidently wrong that it cannot possibly be the real aim the European Union and that it must be the scaremongering propaganda of 'Little Englanders' and reactionary old Tories who still refer to Zimbabwe as Rhodesia. But just listen to what the architects of the European Union say themselves:

"The European Union is currently a state under construction. The construction of one state is its final conclusion."

— *Elmar Brok, Chairman of the European Parliament's Committee on Foreign Affairs*

"The European constitution is as perfect as the constitution of the USA. It will remove all remaining obstacles to the eventual social, political and economic union of this continent. We cannot allow an ideological and unworkable concept of direct democracy to block the creation of the European nation."

— *Valéry Giscard d'Estaing, Ex French President*

"We ought to work on a common constitution to turn the European Union into an entity under international law—that is my goal. It is the decisive task of our time."

— *Joschka Fischer, German Foreign Minister, Berlin, 25 November, 1998.*

"Anyone in Britain who claims the constitution will not change things is trying to sweeten the pill for those who don't want to see a bigger role for Europe. The constitution is not just an intellectual exercise. It will fundamentally alter everything"

— *Former Italian Prime Minister Lamberto Dini, The Sunday Telegraph, 1st June 2003*

If you are still not a little disturbed by these Soviet style megalomanic pronouncements, look at the first sentence of the Treaty of Rome, which founded the European Union. This is single most important declaration and the purpose of the EU summed up in one line.

"Determined to establish the foundations of an ever closer union among the European peoples"

— Treaty establishing the European Economic Community Treaty of Rome, signed 25 March 1957

An *ever* closer union can only mean the eventual formation of one state. If you are opposed to the ultimate creation of one single superstate, then it logically follows that you must be anti-EU. This is its stated aim, in black and white, for all to see.

The emerging EU megastate already has its own parliament, executive, supreme court, currency, flag, anthem and written constitution. In addition it wishes to establish an single army, foreign policy, police force, legal and tax system.

The Euro-federalists' most important claim is that the EU is essential to keep peace in Europe. However, democracies do not have a habit of provoking war, whereas forced or premature conglomerations of disparate nations do (eg the Soviet Union, Yugoslavia, and much of Africa). The Euro-realist model of Europe's democracies retaining their identity, and trading freely together, is less likely to end in conflict than is an undemocratic EU megastate.

It is the greatest democratic tragedy of the United Kingdom that successive governments refuse to give the British people a vote on the matter. This is a hugely important question of national independence, which has to be directly voted on.

European treaties take precedence over Acts of Parliament. So if our Government (the executive) is out-voted in Brussels, our Parliament must still implement the treaty into British law (from Sections 2 & 3 and Schedule 2 of the European Communities Act 1972).

The Treaty also decrees that once Brussels has acquired a power from the nation states, that power is never given back (the 'acquis communautaire').

There is a naïve assumption amongst many politicians in the United Kingdom that even though the European Union is flawed, by remaining in it we can change it for the better.

THE EU ASSAULT ON INDEPENDENCE

The European Union has 27 member states with very different cultural and political outlooks. Even founding members and established modern democracies like Italy, have a poltical culture unrecognisable from our own. In Britian it would be inconceivable to have polticians in office who had fraud convictions or who passed immunity laws to protect themselves from prosecution. Corruption, cronyism and poltical extemism (both left and right wing) are all far more prevalent in Italy and many other EU states and the idea that the UK can change that institutionalised culture, is fantasy.
As if the EU had not already expanded enough, it intends to also add Turkey (which will become one of the most influential mebers owing to its large population and strategic military importance). There are also long term plans to add the Balkan countries. Unanimity amongst the members will therefore become an increasingly impossible task and the UK's influence over the whole organisation will be weakened.

Very soon, we will have to choose.

Do we want to become the subservient region of one federal state, or do we want to stand on our own feet and take our rightful place in the world?
There is surely nothing frightening, extreme right-wing, or negative about renegotiating our membership (or leaving) and keeping our hard-won right to govern ourselves. It would be a liberating and democratic.

How and why did Britain give up?

"We'll negotiate withdrawal from the EEC"

— *Tony Blair, personal election manifesto for Beaconsfield and Sedgefield (1983)*

1. The Culture of Excessive Management

First, let us consider a major change in the situation of the British since 1945. At that period, we were governed by nothing beyond the elected Commons and the hereditary Lords at Westminster. It is true that we had signed up to various international conventions (about war, traffic and so on) and that we were part of a wider system of international law. But our Government in all essential matters made its own decisions according to a broad judgement of the British national interest. We were sovereign. Sovereignty is not, of course, the same as omnipotence, any more than individualism is a licence for self-indulgence. Britain was a responsible nation and the interests of others were always recognised as having a bearing on our own.
Since 1945, however, we have acquired a remarkable array of additional managers, indeed, layer upon layer of them. To them we have delegated extensive authority to tax and regulate us.
First must be mentioned the vast increase in international instruments associated with the United Nations and other treaties – the Convention on Refugees of 1951[6] for example.

---

[6] The text of this and many other such declarations may be found in Ian Brownlie (ed.)

HOW AND WHY DID BRITIAN GIVE UP?

Acting as what is currently called a "good global citizen" plays well with the British electorate for many reasons, some of which we shall mention later, but it plays especially well with politicians, for whom signing up to abstract principles looks statesman-like.

Statesmen are irresistibly charmed by the fact that any embarrassing consequences of these acts are only likely to become evident after they have retired from office. In other words, signing up to blue sky virtues has become a respectable way of striking grand postures in political life without the fear that embarrassing consequences might follow. Such an erosion of democratic accountability is one way of formulating my fundamental criticism of what is happening to us.
A second layer of management was created in Britain by the New Labour government of 1997, in the form of devolved legislatures with extensive powers which were set up to allow a certain amount of autonomy for Scotland and Wales.

The attempt to create elected regional assemblies in England has so far failed, but all of this constitutional fussing has had its effects on English politics, and many people think the solution would be to create even more layers of management, so that we may have the wisdom of additional elected representatives (serving on Regional Assemblies in England) to help in ordering our lives.[7]
The third and most comprehensive layer of management over us is of course that of the European Union. It has a bureaucracy, and a kind of parliament, but its powers could not for a moment be understood as democratically responsive. Its directives and regulations are recognised as taking precedence over Parliamentary legislation in Britain, and any appeal against them must be heard in its own European Court, in which the literal meaning of the words of an EU law is subordinated

---

Basic Documents on Human Rights, Clarendon Press Oxford, 1971.

[7] The most recent proposal in Britain (The Daily Telegraph 21 March 2008) is to substitute an elected chamber (to be called a Senate) for the current House of Lords. This new layer of representatives, we may guess, would be a great deal more active and interfering than the House of Lords we have inherited from past times.
The name will assimilate our English eccentricity to practices elsewhere. Thomas Hobbes in Leviathan (1651) identified "imitation of neighbour nations" in Ch. 29 as being one danger to constitutional stability.

to their consonance with the basic purpose of the Union. The Commission is a fecund creator of regulations affecting many things in our everyday life, ranging from land-fill disposal of waste to the design of buses on our streets. There is, I think, no satisfactory way to quantify how much of our national life is determined by this body, and estimates vary from ten percent to eighty.

It is certainly true that while in principle the House of Commons should be monitoring this avalanche of legislation, much of it goes through "on the nod", if even that. We shall return to this point. In addition, where doubt arises about how far a directive should reach, the instinct of the British civil service is to make them far more restrictive than the way they commonly operate on the Continent. This is a process known as "gold plating."

We are thus managed as we have never been managed before, and these increases in layers of masters over us have not at all been matched by any corresponding diminution in the numbers of those below.[8]

Managing us is a growth industry, part of an expanding public sector. But when, to ask the naïve question, did anyone ever say: "We need more managers to regulate our lives? They will bring us a great access of wisdom and order"?

We have somehow drifted into this most remarkable situation, and to bring out how remarkable it is, let us indulge in what scientists call a "thought experiment". Imagine if we had found ourselves in precisely this situation in 1939 when the fate of the world depended on Britain's readiness to take a stand. Hitler dominated Germany, Mussolini Italy, Franco was ruler of Spain and France was deeply split.

We need not mention the political alignments of Hungary, Romania and the rest. It is clear that in such a situation, we would have had no

---

[8] Nor indeed, any decline in the cost of these managers. Peter Lilley made the essential point in a brilliant speech in June 2008. He was introducing in the House of Commons a bill to require the Senior Salaries Review Body to take into account the transfers of powers between Parliament and EU institutions when making recommendations on MPs pay. Arguing that as most of the
legislative work in governing Britain is now done in Brussels why should British MPs still get paid the same when their work load was vastly less? Our MPs would, he added, "prefer to claim paternity [of these laws] rather than admit impotence – the fate of the cuckold across the ages."

alternative – at least no legal alternative – but to become a pawn of the Axis powers.

Ah! comes the familiar rejoinder: but that is just the point! The creation of the European Union is a process precisely designed to prevent any such threat to European civilisation ever happening again. By locking Germany and other European countries that have been vulnerable to political folly into a liberal free-trade federation, we are preventing any of those cultures from again going off the rails of decency.
This is the moment when we cannot but observe that our naïve question has merely revealed the naivety of the reply. The essence of this simple faith is the error of constitutional fundamentalism: namely, the belief that a constitutional structure will guarantee a political outcome. We may grant, of course, that Europe is unlikely again to be troubled by the march of jackboots. History does not repeat itself in that way – but insidious repetitions of earlier follies certainly do happen. We cannot know what strange passions will shake other European states – or even indeed our own country – in the times to come. We have, one way or another, certainly solved yesterday's problem; but the real concern is with tomorrow's, or the day after tomorrow's.
The present generation looks safe enough from the threat of violent war arising from within Europe itself, but to be confident of the longer future is folly. Abandoning our independence and self-determination for the promise of a collective wisdom embedded in a heterogeneous collection of bureaucrats is certainly a case of selling one's heritage for a mess of pottage. Aspiration is substituted for reality.

Our situation thus provokes us to ask two central questions. The first is why these new managers and their backers are making a
"power grab" to regulate our lives.

The history of that power grab can be read in the nomenclatural changes in the names of the developing stages of the Treaty of Rome. The EEC became the EC and then the EU. At each stage, the power of Brussels to manage us increased.

The second question is why we have allowed it to happen. By and large, free peoples do not like subjecting themselves to additional rulers and masters, especially those whom they have no realistic way of making accountable. A supplementary question here is why the lower levels of power – our Westminster parliament – should have yielded such power. Rulers usually don't like doing that.

There is a sense in which the first question answers itself: the EU keeps on acquiring power because power is the kind of stuff that people like acquiring. But then we run into an interesting fact about both the EU Parliament and that of Westminster. Their powers are vast, but in an important way, they are curiously
impotent. Modern societies are remarkably complex and not easily ruled. There is a strange kind of unreality about both Westminster and Brussels/Strasbourg in our time, and it can

HOW AND WHY DID BRITIAN GIVE UP?

easily be sensed by wandering around the buildings in which these activities are housed. The paradox is that all this power grabbing has turned out to be self-defeating, leading merely to a vast increase in the work of lawyers, courts and tribunals. Our lives are certainly affected by all this busyness, but it does not produce the clear facilitation of our freedoms that even the legislators would want.

This paradoxical impotence of civil management, as growing more futile the more it covers, lies at the heart of much that is happening today. These flies on the axle wheel of history, unlike Aesop's, know all too well that the dust raised is not the result of their work. Statesmen dealing with serious issues transcend their personal ambitions. Politicians involved in make-believe changes in society soon lose their contact with reality and go in for

expenses manipulation and general nest-feathering. One looks in vain to our political managers at all levels for some sign of

the quality of statesmanship so evident in, for example, the 1935 Commons that took Britain into the Second World War. The vast

expansion of political management that we have endured has had the consequence that most political deliberation in these assemblies has the character of pointless churning. At the same time, the quality of the politico-managerial class has declined to that of merely manipulative political experts in public relations. Looking at the standard of parliamentarians at both Brussels and Westminster, one can hardly resist the view that futility breeds

corruption.

The point can be made in terms both of money and of power. It is a basic principle of human life that any large stock of money attracts corruption the way manure attracts flies. Charitable bequests need careful watching lest the money be misappropriated. Vast amounts of aid have been funnelled to the Third World since 1945, but relatively little of it has reached the ground.

In high taxing democracies, politicians find themselves disposing of vast quantities of money and it is hardly surprising that corruption follows, even in Britain, which has a history of relative probity in its public life.

Most people can be foolish with their own money on occasion, but public money is dispensed by people whose accountability cannot be easily fixed at all. In modern welfare states, employment law ensures that little short of overt criminality can separate a bureaucrat, indeed any employee, from his or her office. Waste and incompetence have become very hard to control.

Turning to the issue of political power, we must concern ourselves with what had better be called a "bureaucratic dynamic". Law as traditionally understood in Britain during modern times signified legislating a framework within which individuals could pursue their own projects, and the result was a society that was imitated the world over. In our generation, however, governments seldom pass "laws" in the strict sense. Rather they send "messages", mandate targets, attempt to change cultures by fiscal policy, seek to "solve the problems of ordinary people" and in other ways try to micromanage their subjects. Identifying an evil (child abuse, professional misconduct and suchlike things) provokes regulations that impose sanctions upon malefactors. But regulation drives out the self-monitoring integrity that previously governed the conduct of self-governing professionals, such as doctors and lawyers. Parents are similarly corrupted. Codification of the rules of decency in any area turns those newly subject to such powers into employees. When professional life is governed by integrity, individuals may often mistake their selfish desires for a higher calling, but the idea that external regulation with sanctions prevents, or even much reduces, evil is false.

It merely leads to casuistry and teaches evil how to exploit the arts of evasion.

The standard political diagnosis of regulation-failure is always that the regulations did not go far enough, and the solution is to

HOW AND WHY DID BRITIAN GIVE UP?

take further powers to control the newly revealed imperfections. The bureaucracy issues new regulations, which
in turn suffer the same fate as before. In many cases, this follow up regulation is needed to withdraw the bad effects of many of the earlier reforms. We have here, then, a feedback loop in which
political meddling merely increases its reach without achieving its ambition. This is the bureaucratic dynamic of contemporary micromanagement, and it is demeaning for the masters no less than it is for those subject to it.

THE END OF ENGLAND

2. Sources of Servility

That we in Britain should be subject to this multiplying managerialism suggests to me that Britons are becoming a servile people, eager to accept the yoke.
I think that such feebleness is part of the spirit of the age in which we live, a readiness to surrender independence in exchange for subsidy and help in living our lives.
But to recognise this development as the servility it actually is would be painful to many people. Moral degeneration must be presented in more palatable ways by those who intend to profit by it. In what way has it been made palatable?

The answer is that submission to more and more authority comes dressed as virtue. From about 1918 onwards, high-toned Western politicians have often made speeches arguing that "national sovereignty" was an outmoded and possibly dangerous idea. The great thing was international regulation of inter-state relations, the emerging system that has come to be euphemistically called "global governance".

This euphemism is designed to suggest (quite falsely) that the regulations constituting the "governance" have been untouched by any human concerns with interest or with power. They have merely emerged, as it were, from the necessities of bringing justice out of anarchy. Between the wars, the League of Nations

was the vehicle of these illusions, and after the Second World War, it was the United Nations. Rejection of national sovereignty and the vogue for treating the United Nations as a legal and moral rather than merely a political body was part of a more general movement suggesting that the authority of international bureaucrats was less tainted by national partiality (and thus more rational) than the decisions of nation states.

HOW AND WHY DID BRITIAN GIVE UP?

The plausibility of this argument depends partly on a philosophical mistake, which is to identify nationalism with the national interest.
"Nationalism" here is wrongly used to cover everything from separatist movements such as those of the Basques and the Irish Republicans to aggressive national policies such as those of Hitler and Mussolini. But neither of these latter figures was
a nationalist in the true sense. Hitler believed in race, which is quite different from nation, and Mussolini was a socialist who invented a solidarist doctrine he called "totalitarianism", and also "fascism". The national interest of countries such as Britain and France, by contrast, rests upon quite distinct and non-ideological considerations. It incorporates, or at least can and often does incorporate, a wider concern for the interests of other states. Neither of these political calculations – nationalism, or the
national interest - is necessarily bad, or indeed good either, but misunderstood in this way, both serve to generate what we may call "the internationalist illusion", which is the belief that international politicians and bureaucrats are wiser than those of (for example) European national states.
Anyone who actually believes this should look upon the UN and the EU, and despair.
Yet even those who do look at the record of these remarkable organisations, and despair, will often support them, partly because they think that in so doing they are behaving like good global citizens and thus being models that may, so it is hoped, influence the unregenerate brutes ruling countries in which human rights are not taken seriously.

The idea is that internationality is the wisdom of the future, and that even if the current record of international organisation is hardly to be admired, this is where the future lies. Such ideas are often sustained by pseudo-philosophical forms of collective self-hatred directed at the whole history of our civilisation.
We shall return to this theme in sections (5) and (6).

3. Complexity and Accountability

Let us return to our basic question: why is it that we should be subject to so many layers of managerial regulation? Why, particularly, given that we look at these political managers and often curl our lips in derision, have we found ourselves at
their mercy? Our derision turns out to be no protection against being staked out, like Gulliver, by all these meddling Liliputions.
A common answer is that the modern world has become so complex that it requires increasing quantities of central direction. We get new layers of management because we need them. Everywhere in the modern world we look (so 'tis said) we find what economists call "externalities". These are incidental evils created by legitimate activities, and they are things that require to be regulated in the name of justice. Noise, the disposal of waste, the capitalist weakness for colluding with competitors over price, the caprice of employers, the emergence of monopolies,
the protection of workers from unfair competition – a regulator's work is never done!

Such central direction, however, was a thesis tested to destruction in the Soviet Union and other communist states, and then further tested in the welfare managerialism of the 1970s. In both of these cases, governments responding to the complexity of society made a great mess of their tasks, and began to destroy
the prosperity on which their power depended.

There is a contrary argument which free market liberals advance against this passion to have our troubles resolved by regulation. It advances the opposite case - that the more complex a society becomes, the less need there is to regulate it.
A club, or a household, or a firm may be regulated minutely if the responsible people choose because the members all share, or
seem to share, a single interest in the success of the enterprise.

HOW AND WHY DID BRITIAN GIVE UP?

The point of "society" as a whole, however, is that it does not have a single enterprise, or common interest, except, perhaps, the formal interest free peoples have in being governed by law rather than command. Hence the more complex societies become, the less regulation they will need – so long, that is to say, as we assume that the individual members of society are competent to manage their own lives. And that assumption, of course, is the central issue.

The justification for a welfare state taking over so many of the functions that in earlier times were done by individuals themselves – health, education, security etc. – was that some people were poor, or underprivileged, or not educated enough to manage their own lives, and the state had to do it for them. In time, women, and ethnic minorities, and homosexuals and others found it advantageous to enrol themselves in these "victim classes" of the vulnerable, in need of state agencies to support and protect them. It has become a major change in British life.

Can it now be that most of the British population has been persuaded to recognise that it has lost the competence necessary to manage its own lives, a competence its parents certainly had? Can this be the fundamental belief on which the current apathy and sheep-like quality of the British depends?

Is this the real source of our readiness to put ourselves under the regulation of unaccountable international bodies? This becomes the central question to be considered in this argument.

Perhaps sheer lack of nerve is part of it. But another part is the political use of complexity as a tool of bafflement in persuading some people that these matters are too difficult for them to understand. Complexity is of immense value to politicians and bureaucrats who are kind enough to take off our hands the irksome business of trying to understand – for example! – the real meaning of the Lisbon Treaty. That the people would not
understand its significance has been advanced as a reason for not

holding a referendum on the Treaty. The Liberal Democrats who held this remarkable opinion did think that there might be a case for holding a referendum on the much more general question of whether Britain ought to stay in the European Union or secede from it.

One can easily follow the cunning of such a move, but it has so many deceitful aspects that criticism would hardly know where to start. Is the grand issue of secession really less complex than the question of a current change in the terms of the Union? It is a deadly point in EU polemic that the American constitution is a few pages of limpid prose while European constitutional arrangements are humanly impenetrable.

This is, I think, the decisive proof that the complexity ploy has been a standard tool of deception used by European integrators.
We are throughout dealing, it will be obvious, with fraud, which consists of separating people from some valuable property they own. In this case, the property is our national autonomy and independence. The basic way of defrauding people is to persuade them that the issue is the one the fraudster is explaining to them, whereas in fact the real point of the exercise lies out of sight.

In the case of the European Union, the explicit concern is with ideals – unity, harmonisation, guaranteeing peace in Europe – but
the real issue is power. By focussing on ideals, and flattering as virtuous and realistic those who support them, the rising international managerial class advances in the world.

There is a rather simple variant of fraud that used to happen on street corners, known as the "three-thimble trick". The fraudster has a pea and moves the three thimbles around very fast, inviting the punter to bet on the thimble containing the pea.

The trick may not be sophisticated, but it's a living. The Brussels version of the three-thimble trick is to conceal power under a changing variety of names. In what sense if any, is the European project the same thing as the British seemed to approve in the 1975 referendum? Is it merely an association of like-minded states for limited purposes, or is it the creation of a new state in the world – having, as the Lisbon Treaty makes clear, its own President and its own Foreign Minister?

HOW AND WHY DID BRITIAN GIVE UP?

The deception consists in switching these possibilities according to political convenience, and the only sure fact is that many of the answers to these questions are lies.[9]

And it is necessary to be clear on these points, because the history of deception stretches back to the beginning of Britain's involvement with the European Union.

Politicians in Britain insisted in 1975 that it was merely a device for freeing trade between European states – only, after the referendum, did many of them (led by Edward Heath) pour scorn on this idea because "everybody always knew" that it involved wider ambitions – though it took some time before "ever closer union" became recognised in Britain as the interestingly limitless aim of the association.

The complexity issue brings us back to that of democracy. In a democracy, politicians are accountable for the decisions they take, but in modern highly regulated welfare states, governmental initiatives and policies come so thick and fast that it is extraordinarily difficult to pin responsibility on anyone. We are, as the poet Eliot put it, "distracted by distraction from distraction".

---

[9] A thoughtful and impressive treatment of this general theme may be found in Peter Oborne, *The Rise of Political Lying*, The Free Press: London, 2005. For a detailed history of deception in relations with the EU, the basic text is, Christopher Booker and Richard North, *The Great Deception: A Secret History of the European Union*, Continuum: London, 2003.

THE END OF ENGLAND

It has become the custom in the House of Commons for Ministers presiding over a disaster to say (as for example Charles Clarke said when the Home Office lost sight of 1,000 foreign criminals who ought to have been deported at the end of their prison sentences) "I take full responsibility for this".
But full responsibility would have meant resignation, and he seemed to think, as so many others have in recent administrations, that one can declare oneself responsible and then – as Clarke himself wanted to do – remain in power to clean up the problem. But in the end, what actually happened to those lost criminals?

New stories took our attention. The point of the thing called "spin" is to conceal these embarrassments from public concern – or, as was said infamously said by a Labour aide on the Twin Towers attack, "to bury them".

Prime Minister Blair responded to Britain's revolving presidency of the EU by giving up part of the rebate in our contribution to the Common Agricultural Policy that Margaret Thatcher had achieved at Fontainbleau in 1984.
He did it in exchange for a French promise to "review" the working of the CAP. A promise, however, is an empty thing unless it has consequences. Blair is gone, but we in Britain certainly pay out as a consequence of his riskless generosity.

Quinquennial elections have in our time turned out to be useless in making our rulers accountable to us. Let me suggest, then, that British democracy needs a new principle of accountability, a principle that would respond to the fact that so many worthless declarations are made by modern politicians in their justifications of expensive follies.

HOW AND WHY DID BRITIAN GIVE UP?

My proposal is: that any decision whose point depends upon a prediction of its outcome should be clarified so that the politician making the decision can be held to account. A Commission might well be needed to agree and specify the conditions of the political decision. And by "held to account" I mean that the failure of the decision to generate the consequences predicted should lead to his (or her) immediate fall from office and from parliament.

In many cases no doubt, the consequences might not become evident until the relevant officeholder had retired, or had died. In that case, such figures would be subject to an appropriate form of denigration and obloquy. The reason so much of our politics is light-minded is that lying to us is a costless exercise, and the media, aggressive as they often are, are not very good in their role as keepers of memory.

THE END OF ENGLAND

4. The Lisbon Treaty

The collapse of democratic accountability in contemporary states is partly explained, of course, by the level of deceit on which contemporary politics depends.
Gordon Brown as Prime Minister is, as we earlier remarked, indelibly stained by the cowardly and evasive manner in which he has tried to get round the implications
of Labour's Manifesto commitment to hold a referendum on the Lisbon Treaty. That the Treaty is merely the rejected constitution re-described is almost universally accepted on the Continent, and thus passing it into law after democratic referenda in France and the Netherlands had rejected it is merely one further instance of
the Union's familiar tactic of overriding democratic inconveniences by wearing opposition down. The Brussels oligarchy has a remarkable capacity to make the process move only in the direction of increasing its own power. Jean-Claude Juncker, the premier of Luxembourg, put the essence of the matter quite crisply, "of course there will be transfers of sovereignty", he remarked, but added that he would not want to draw the attention of the British public to this fact.

"There is", he went on to remark about the Treaty, "a single legal personality for the EU, the primacy of European law, a new architecture for foreign and security policy, there is an enormous extension in the fields of the EU's powers, there is the Charter of Fundamental Rights..."[10]

British politicians, however, lie to us in claiming more solidity than they can sustain for the "red lines" exempting Britain from a variety of Treaty commitments. The Commission merely waits patiently for more pliable politicians who can be quietly persuaded to modify and eventually abandon any such

---

[10] The Daily Telegraph, July 3, 2007.

limitations. And there is no real accountability for the likely collapse of these reservations when the European Court of Justice gets to work on the Treaty.

Sometimes the deceptions are contained in absurd formulations so rhetorically confused that they seem to turn a negative into a positive. The idea of "pooling sovereignty" for example, suggests positive harmony and cooperation but what it actually means is that Britain gives up its sovereignty on the issues in question, and
agrees to be bound by a new sovereign in the form of EU machinery in which it has but a part, and in a 27 member association, a rather small part. If this machinery produces a decision we do not like, we have lost our independence and can do nothing about it.

The issues are complex, and are detailed in a 63,000 word document presented as a series of amendments to the existing treaties, and before I broach the central cultural question, I want to make two observations. The first is to point to one notable example of constitutional betrayal, and the other is to highlight the fundamental cultural difference between Britain and the Continent.

The constitutional betrayal relates to individual liberty. In 2007, a deal was proposed to send back to their countries of origin the 2,000 EU prisoners in British jails, in exchange for allowing the 800 British subjects said to be in Continental jails to finish their sentences in Britain. This would help Britain in dealing with its major crisis with prison provision in Britain. However the Parliamentary European Scrutiny Committee wrote to Joan Ryan, then the relevant Home Office Minister, to point out that a British subject (such as David Irving who had been jailed for Holocaust Denial in Austria) could then be transferred to a British prison to serve time for something that was not a crime in Britain. Such a problem might have been met by a principle of dual criminality, but the UK had earlier abandoned that principle for thirty-two offences when it had agreed the European arrest warrant three years earlier. The Parliamentary Committee thought this issue important enough to warrant a parliamentary debate and placed a "scrutiny reserve" on the proposed agreement. The point of such a scrutiny reserve is that a proposed directive should be debated in Parliament itself before Britain would agree to it. Later in 2007, however, a deal was struck at the EU Justice and Home Affairs Council meeting attended by Ms. Ryan. Like other spineless British ministers, she took no notice of the scrutiny reserve, and went along with the majority supporting, with no concern for safeguards, the proposal for exchanging the prisoners. Her boss, the Home Secretary at the time John Reid approved the deal as good for Britain, and the Scrutiny Committee was revealed as unable to protect our liberties from the overwhelming power of a united EU bureaucracy.[11]

There would, of course, be one way in which this kind of conflict might be avoided. It would be for Britain to fall into line with some other European states by making Holocaust Denial a crime in Britain, and dear ingenious Angel Merkel actually did make this helpful suggestion. In doing so, she was exhibiting the deep Continental instinct for solving problems by "harmonisation." And that brings me to the second point.

It is that Britain is in its constitutional life and culture a major exception to many Continental practices. This is why Continental

---

[11] I am indebted to a brilliant account of this process by Philip Johnston in The Daily Telegraph 7 April, 2007. The point obviously does not involve anything as absurd as defending David Irving and Holocaust Denial. As Johnston points out, had such a law been operational in Britain, Prince Harry would have been in trouble over his swastika kit for a fancy dress party.

countries since the eighteenth century have recognised her as a model of a free society, by contrast with the Napoleonic and Prussian traditions of the Rechtsstaat in most of Europe. European states are certainly free, but they are also responsive to the demands of an intrusive bureaucracy in a way that the British used not to be. These states contain, of course, immensely powerful antipathies that must be accommodated by the conventions of a debate between Government and Opposition, conventions that have been adapted from British practice, but their ideal is one of national harmony in which subjects accept the basic structure of the state and all pull together. The jury system is not at home in such a world and the natural mode of understanding the place of the individual is in terms of rights. The English tradition of freedom, by contrast, long resisted the assimilation of its tradition of freedom to the codification of rights.

John Locke had, of course, talked of natural rights, using the idea as a casual philosophical way of formulating English freedom, but his ideas were turned to another purpose by Continental followers. A schedule of rights adumbrates a correct ordering of society, whereas English freedom contains built in limitations

to freedom, and facilitates a changing cultural character responsive in each generation to the changing tastes and ideas of the people. English life, in other words is based upon a conflict model of society whose stability results not from a process of "harmonisation" but from a tension between balanced desirabilities in an ambivalent world: between competing business firms, for example, political parties, prosecution and defence in trials, versions of faiths and so on.

The basic British objection to the way in which the European project accommodates Britain is that British life has become subject to an alien tradition. The conflict between metric and imperial measures is merely a dramatic symbol of this conflict,

but versions of it will be found at all levels of our involvement with Europe, and its essence lies in the European passion to harmonise us into little Europeans. The rest – the hideous costs, the destruction of our fishing waters, the corruption of the Brussels bureaucracy, the waste of the CAP – these things are important, but they are not the heart of the matter.

HOW AND WHY DID BRITIAN GIVE UP?

5. Folie á Deux

Analysing some of the processes and the deceptions that have brought us to our present enfeebled condition is a depressing business. A great nation making its way in the world has, over the last half century, abandoned its own unique integrity
because it feared isolation and fell into cultural confusion. Given its cultural vitality and its global reach, Britain was perhaps the last country in the world that might find itself "isolated". It has a Commonwealth and a special relationship with an Anglosphere, for a start. Australia in one way, Singapore in another and Canada in yet another are examples of countries that have prospered economically without losing their nerve and therefore having to compromise their political independence.

Yet one of the world's top five or six economies sold itself into alien management because fools had persuaded it that only the big battalions could survive in the emerging world of the twenty first century. It finds itself locked into an association marked by timid protectionism and demographic decline. A whole political class has been found wanting, and as a result of failing the test of courage, that class has fallen into the trivialities of corruption and self-seeking.

Unfortunately it must be said that we get the rulers that we deserve. "We" – meaning a large section of the electorate – have been told that "our" dependence on the state is the proper response to a world of unequal advantages, and "we" have believed what "we" were told. To make every transaction pass some test of justice seemed to have entailed dependence on a regulating state. The result has been that many Britons have acquired the notion that the income they earn is
pocket money to be spent on the satisfaction of their current wants, rather than resources to be managed in terms of present and future contingencies.

Similarly, when they worry about "the work-life balance", they are dreaming that the week might be turned into an interminable weekend. There are always richer "others" whose taxes can pay for all those things the state provides, and in our time, the state has ranged so far into the enterprises of civil society that virtually nothing has not become in some degree subsidised, and therefore, in a little time, controlled by the state. At the same time, "we" have also learned that pains can mostly be abolished, "pains" here signifying anything ranging from punishment in schools to losing one's job as a result of incompetence. We have come to think, as PJ O'Rourke put it, that we may "vote ourselves rich". And the result is that we expect politicians to bribe us.

Issues that are situated beyond this immediate concern with "the things that affect people's lives" are of little concern for a large part of the electorate.

The importance of our national independence happens to be one of them. And, of course, it is by far the most important.

We critics might well despise our political class as corrupt and mediocre, but the vital point is that we must recognise that the situation is one of folie á deux.

A population persuaded by the rhetoric that generates its dependent condition has become, by the device of the focus group, the yardstick of what politicians ought to be doing.

They may talk (God help us!) of "visions", but their minds are largely circumscribed by the thought of the next election. They think they should be offering what the demos wants, or (not at all the same thing) what it says it wants. In no political party these days do we have more than a handful of politicians prepared
to challenge the remarkable mind-set of our time in the name of reality.

And until a class of politicians ready to do this emerges to save us (if it ever does), we shall be forever drifting in the political pidgin talk that constitutes the relationship between Westminster and its electors.

HOW AND WHY DID BRITIAN GIVE UP?

6. Conceptualising the Collapse

Let me end by sketching out a schema that might be one possible way of exploring how the people of Britain have fallen into this sad condition. Some theologians used to talk about "spilt religion", but I think we should look at "spilt idealism".

Idealism is a form of moral energy that we invest in some way of life, in our moral admirations and in our sense, for example, of the kind of conduct that is "below us".

Most Europeans, indeed probably most collective groups, invest a good deal of their idealism in their own national identity, believing that the nation stands for many admirable things.

Occasionally they invest it in other nations, as some Britons did,
for example, who came to have a remarkable admiration for Wilhelmine Germany in the late nineteenth century – Houston Stewart Chamberlain and Winifred Wagner, for example. In the ideological passions of the twentieth century, a lot of British
idealism was invested in the Soviet Union, and some in Fascism and Nazism.

Mostly however, idealism stays home. Milton talked about "God's Englishmen" while many Edwardians thought that being born British was to have won first prize in the lottery of life.
These are marvellous exhibitions of a kind of national arrogance, but today many Britons actually think we are much worse than other peoples. And this kind of posturing humility is one aspect of the collapse of idealism in Britain, because although arrogance may be a fault, it is also the indispensable source of a number of interesting and indispensable virtues.

THE END OF ENGLAND

It stands behind the belief, for example, that being English/British is a form of responsibility requiring self-control in the presence of foreigners. "Remember you're British" has now degenerated into a joke expression, but a generation or two
back, it represented an element in the moral core of British people. In those happier times, the image of the Englishman abroad was that of the gentleman.
Such an image was sustained in times past by the sense of patriotic self-regard very common among Britons travelling abroad.

There is much less patriotism around today, with the result that young British people have been liberated from any sense of national responsibility, and with their drunken and vomiting ways, are currently feared and despised in places as distant as Bangkok and Benidorm.

What seems to have happened, then, is a withdrawal of British investment of idealism in being British. That investment in the past would be signalled by pride in anything from Shakespeare and Nelson to a propensity for queuing or the reputation of the BBC. People can be proud of a whole range of things, both national and individual, for any number of reasons good or bad, and any serious form of pride carries responsibility with it. This withdrawal of pride in being British has several significant aspects. One of them is that admiration for our achievements has been replaced by a schedule of shames, from indulgence in the slave trade before 1807 to the Crusades, the Irish famine, or whatever other set of events the critic might choose.

Another aspect is that many people have simply switched their admirations away from a British identity to some narrower focus in which admiration is entangled with a sense of grievance.

HOW AND WHY DID BRITIAN GIVE UP?

Society in this way has been atomised. Feminists, for example, replace admiration for being British by disdain for what are taken to be the patriarchal power structures thought to characterise earlier times.
Again, some members of ethnic groups in Britain have demanded that their own particular glories ought to be celebrated as part of a multicultural mosaic. A whole underworld of grievances is cultivated in this area, but it is relatively marginal compared to something much more fundamental.

Many who reject Britain interpret any sense of national superiority as involving aggression and xenophobia. These people think that if Britons could be persuaded to abandon pride in Britishness and adopt a more realistic humility, they would as a result be more internationally peaceful. Whether the British have a notable addiction to being aggressive is no doubt an arguable matter, but the charge of xenophobia has no basis at all in reality. On the contrary, Britons have exhibited interest in and sympathy for most of the peoples of the world. In European politics, the claims of the kings of England to be also kings of France were a notable source of warlike aggression, but those follies ended in the sixteenth century, after which national policy was never purely and unambiguously aggressive.

Like all other Europeans, the British are ambivalent in their attitudes to Germans, French, Dutch and the rest but the notion that they would be nicer if the history books were rewritten so that Agincourt and Trafalgar were cast out of the national memory is evidently absurd.

I say these elementary things merely to clear away some of the modish nonsense of the time, and it brings me to the basic point.

THE END OF ENGLAND

British idealism has been withdrawn from the British tradition itself and invested in an abstract ideal world whose most conspicuous reality (to the extent that it is real at all) is to be found in international organisations such as the UN and the EU.

This is a safe if somewhat feeble option, because these organisations seldom have to take any decisive action, as nation
states must do, and they limit their activities to taking up virtuous postures. Who could be embarrassed by a virtuous posture? Nation states, by contrast, must often act, and sometimes do so inadvisedly, as the British did over Suez in 1956, and many would add, over Iraq in 2003. This asymmetry between real centres of power and aspirational moral entities helps to sustain the idea that codifications of rights and international organisations represent a wisdom not available to national states which are subject to the distorting partialities of the national interest.
The intellectual source of this curious distortion of idealism as a moral investment is to be found in the world of pedagogy. Universities, in the twentieth century especially, took up the idea that their academic essence was to be critical, and this plausible but misleading abstraction led many to think that serious seekers after truth must detach themselves from local political and religious beliefs in order to locate themselves in an innocent and guiltless "nowhere". These people became, as it were, the patriots of Geneva, the Hague or the New York of the UN.

This is a stance supplying the agreeably self-congratulatory option of thinking oneself "above" the vulgar prejudices of patriots and ordinary people.
Schoolteachers are another notable source of this moral disinvestment of idealism in Britain.
Many explicitly regard patriotism as vulgar, and "criticism" means reading the past with hindsight through the lens of current moral fashions.

HOW AND WHY DID BRITIAN GIVE UP?

The result is to discover that our ancestors were, unfortunately, not up to our standards. The old British arrogance, rejected when based upon our national tradition reappears as pedagogic self-congratulation about a kind of unreal moral superiority. It is a
posture depending upon the belief that we in our time, or perhaps merely these critical believers themselves, have attained a perfection of moral understanding.

The simplicity of mind sometimes to be found in contemporary pedagogy is quite remarkable. A sketch can barely touch the complexity of this long development, but one may mention one or two of its better-known aspects.
One of them is the ethical relativism widely current in the early twentieth century. These were doctrines that fed into a more general pseudo-philosophical scepticism which has often been combined with a straightforward dogmatism about current moral opinions, on rights, equality and justice for example.

Another component is the post-modernist belief that truth is the handmaiden of power, and hence that truth and objectivity are not to be known (if, indeed, they are not merely tools of masculinist ideology).
Multiculturalism in this context despises the common beliefs of the Western tradition (Christianity, progress, the value of technology, for example) but reveres the practices of other cultures as a necessary correction of European arrogance in past times. Truth in much of this world is replaced by discourse analysis and literature is often treated merely as a revelation of the unjust power structures of earlier times.

Human beliefs are usually sustained by some degree of self-congratulation.
Those who have withdrawn their investment of idealism in Britain and taken up internationality on the one hand, and a

mechanical scepticism/dogmatism on the other, congratulate themselves on not being prejudiced as others are. They have
been liberated from the cage of convention into the broad pastures of reason. Part of the public relations of this set of notionally critical beliefs is that the believers have triumphed by hard struggle over the overpowering conventions of a repressive
Christian and capitalist civilisation.

Here, then, we have one of the many famous ways in which peoples are victimised by illusion. They may be the merest sheep
picking up fashionable doctrines, but they imagine themselves as lions who have triumphed over an imprisoning mind set. This is, of course, a new version of an old indoctrination.

Hitler turned the German population into sheep by explaining to
them that, merely by virtue of their race, they were lions.
My suggestion is, then, that the sheep-like indifference of much of the articulate element of the British population to the loss of its historical autonomy may be explained in terms of spilt
idealism: specifically, the transfer of admiration from our national traditions to that of a guiltless internationality. The consequences of this curious mistake are no doubt a good deal less serious than was the case with those who in the last century invested idealism in appalling ideologies, but this internationalist enthusiasm has itself a special problem. International organisations and declarations of rights are unreal repositories of admiration.

As unreal entities, international organisations lack concrete particularity. They are a kind of phantom or substitute commitment, and the consequences of this are by no means unfamiliar to both psychologists and political scientists.

HOW AND WHY DID BRITIAN GIVE UP?

Commitment to a guiltless perfection lacks the discipline inseparable from a real moral investment.
The result is a curious split in the moral life. Psychoanalysts have often been preoccupied with a split in the love life of neurotic men whose idealism about women can recognise in the feminine nothing except the figures of the mother and the whore.

Such a split turns reality into fantasy. Again, the ideal intentions of ideological rulers impelled them to behave in the most deceitful and ruthless ways, good purposes being taken to justify any murderousness deemed necessary to the cause.

Similarly, the investment of idealism in such unreal phantoms as international organisations leads to a parallel split, in this case a split between high toned postures on the one hand, and a drifting avoidance of real commitment on the other.

The very image of this kind of split may be found in the famous concert in 2007 designed to help "make poverty history" in the Third World, but especially in Africa. This is a posture of remarkable ambition – the transformation of the condition of millions of people.
These Britons, mostly young, have ambitions about transforming the world that are little short of megalomania.

Their claim on virtue consists in passionate support for development aid to the needy, an end to war, a banning of land mines, a reduction of carbon emissions and the rest of the current causes of our time, but in their private lives their capacity to defer gratification, control their impulses, resist drugs and debt, recognise duties and stick to commitments is often remarkably defective. And the connection between these two attitudes is that the sense of virtue attached to the idealistic posturing seems to licence a certain insouciance in lesser matters of personal life. Many of these people live in a kind of perpetual childhood, and once they have lost the security of the parental home, many of them live alone because solitude least interferes with the uncluttered life devoted to satisfying impulses.

If I am right about the consequences of an idealism that has been invested in a riskless and therefore unreal perfection, then the widespread indifference among Britons to the dangers of Britain abandoning democracy in favour of submission to a benevolent oligarchy in Brussels would cease to be mysterious. The mediocrity of our politics, and of our political class, would result from the fact that a large component of the British population, especially among the educated, can only recognise two concerns. One is the grand and slightly mad project of perfecting the world, and the other is the search for personal happiness and satisfaction.

The real world of politics, however, is about grander issues of national interest in the here and now and many of our contemporaries are so lost in posturing unrealities of global perfectionism on the one hand, and the demands of immediate personal satisfaction on the other, that they lack even the capacity to recognise much less to respond to the political realities that are shaping Britain's future.

What now for England's Green and Pleasant Land?

"England expects that every man will do his duty" — *Admiral Horatio Nelson at the Battle of Trafalgar, shortly before being killed (21st October 1805)*

As things currently stand none of the main parties in the United Kingdom are willing to promote any policies which promote a genuinely British, or English identity. Nor are any of the parties willing to regain genuine independence from the European Union, or halt mass immigration from the developing world.

The rise of a new mainstream party advocating these policies is a virtual impossibility given the "first-past-the-post" electoral system which disproportionately favours the established parties.

The Green Party and the United Kingdom Independence Party gained almost one million combined votes at the last election, yet they were not given one MP between them. Including the votes given to other smaller parties, that means that more than one million voters remain totally unrepresented in parliament.

The "first-past-the-post" system combined with the sociological inertia of electors and tribal loyalties, means that the Conservatives and Labour are the only parties who will ever win in the UK in the forseeable future.

THE END OF ENGLAND

Who then shall speak for England?

The Conservative Party offers the only practical hope of defending the British, and particularly English, identity. Labour and the Liberal Democrats are commited to multiculturalism, a policy of limited immigration controls and they are keen on Euro-federalism.

Both parties also have a disproportionate dependency on Scottish and Welsh votes, so are particularly unwilling to promote an English identity. As we have also seen, Labour gain much from the Muslim block-vote.

The only pragmatic solution is that the disparate factions in the Centre and on the Right must unite within the Conservative Party rather than fighting on the fringes like the United Kingdom Independence Party (UKIP). Worse still, we must not allow apathy to set in, so that only parties like the British National Party (BNP) monopolise the discussion on mass immigration. This does a disservice to Conservatism and serves to fuel socialist anxiety and hysteria about discussing immigration.

Parties like the BNP and UKIP only exist, because the Conservative Party are not distinguishing themselves from Labour and are not confident enough to discuss the problems brought by mass immigration or the European Union leaving many English people feeling disenfranchised and resentful.

The English should not be afraid of national feeling. Let them ask themselves why should all peoples except the English be encouraged to celebrate and defend their ethnicity?

There is a huge difference between non-aggressive and aggressive patriotism; between those who wish to celebrate and protect their nation within their existing territory and those who wish to invade and compromise the culture and territories of others. The modern English of all peoples can be trusted to remain within the limits of non-aggressive patriotism.The English must work unceasingly to defend their identity and traditions. Defending English identity is not about preserving a nostalgic and rose-tinted *Brideshead Revisited* conception of England. It is about defending the values of moral integrity and intellectual advancement for which this country has traditionally been admired.

www.ingramcontent.com/pod-product-compliance
Ingram Content Group UK Ltd.
Pitfield, Milton Keynes, MK11 3LW, UK
UKHW041434180426
11947UKWH00007B/433